'1 50

Volume #2
only

The Supreme Master Ching Hai

Love Love

For Butterfly

and Peter, the stray well-mannered dog

For the dogs in my life

And all the animals alike

Despite the fact that we are an odd herd

with different species of dogs,

we all have one thing in common —

this beloved human "pet," we all own!

Inspired by the dogs

Compiled by

Supreme Master Ching Hai

And to all the dogs that I love:

1 Benny

2 Lucky

3 Happy

4 Hermit

5 Goody

6 Boyo

7 Lady

8 Pomas

9 Zolo

10 Hally

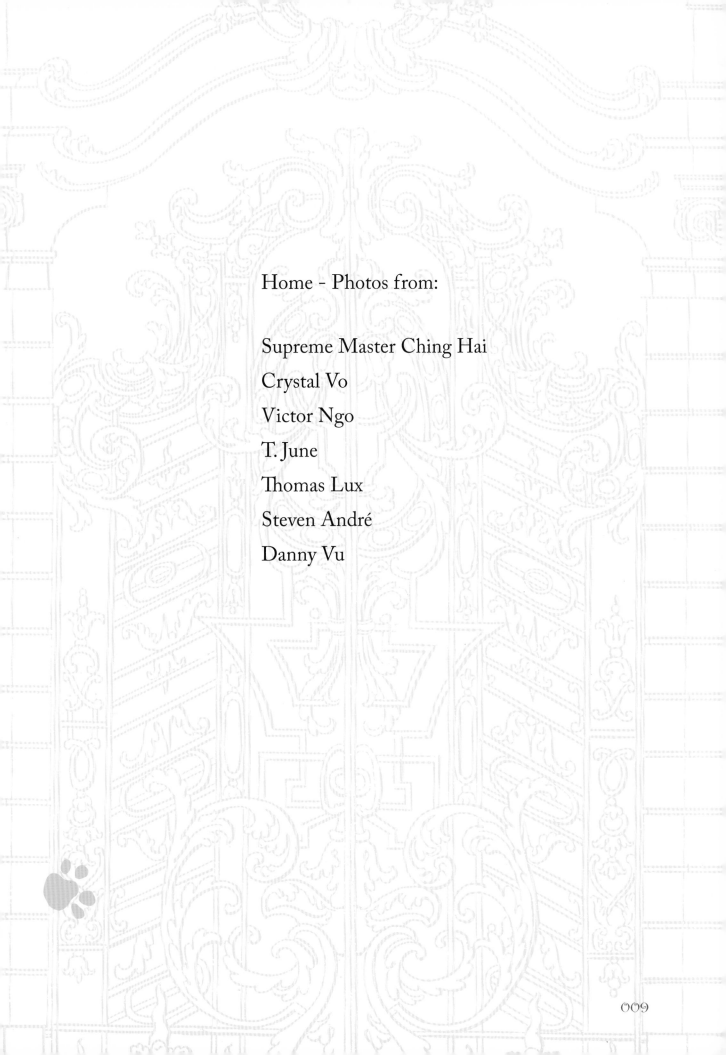

Home - Photos from:

Supreme Master Ching Hai

Crystal Vo

Victor Ngo

T. June

Thomas Lux

Steven André

Danny Vu

Words from a Child

These are the examples of what should be
The life of our friends, sweet animals.
Be it on land, on air or in the sea.
They should be loved, protected and cherished,
Just like the life that we so wish.

Dearest Heaven, Dear Lord of Karma
Please do love and care for all creatures
For it breaks my heart to see their plight.
I cannot bear to see them suffer.

There're plenty places in Heaven above
Take them all up, and give them love.
This's my little prayer for all beings:

Just your little Love and Compassion.
May all be well, live and let live.
All Love, all care and all forgive.

~ Supreme Master Ching Hai

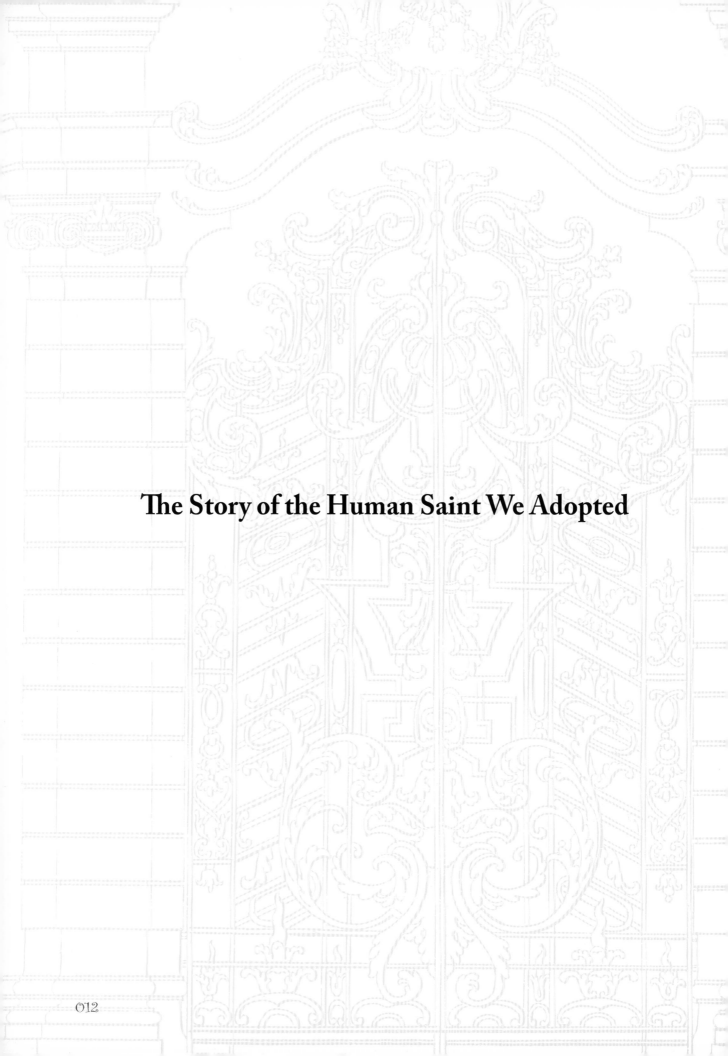

The Story of the Human Saint We Adopted

Collectively written by Ten Lucky Canines

Benny, Lucky, Happy, Hermit, Goody, Boyo, Lady, Pomas, Zolo, and Hally
~ Compiled by Book Group

Our beloved human, or simply, our Mom, is also known by countless people in the world as Supreme Master Ching Hai. As a young child, She already showed signs that She was destined to become a Saint through Her natural great love for all beings, including us animals.

Since becoming an enlightened Master, She has devoted Herself to the teaching of the Quan Yin Method (an ancient meditation practice focusing on the inner Sound and Light) and the promotion of vegetarianism. She once said that if only one half of the world's people became vegetarians, we would have peace on Earth. The killing of animals for food has culminated in a violent atmosphere, which in turn sprouts violence, wars and misery among humans. Therefore, the lives of us animals and those of humanity cannot be separated.

To those who follow our human Saint, She might be a Master or a great teacher, but to us animals, She is just our loving Mom. She does all things a Mom does, like bathing us, cooking for us, singing to us, taking us for walks, and playing with us. We hope we can share Her love with all our animal friends in the world, and that the day will come when each and every one can live a life with an abundance of food, warm shelter, and love, the way we do.

With much love
To Humans and all.

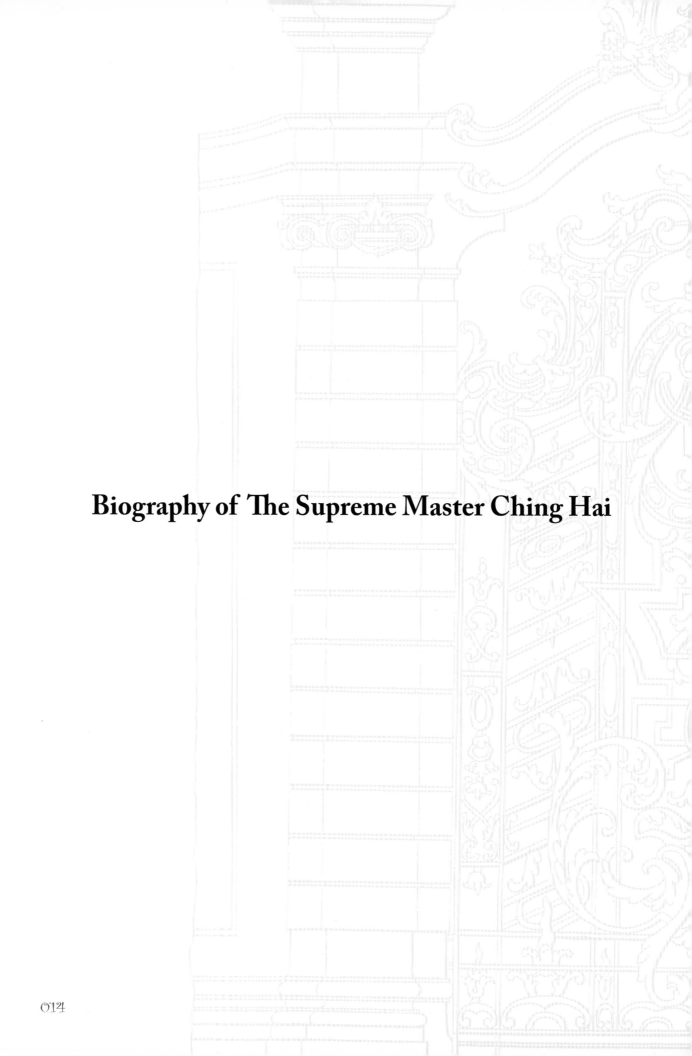

Biography of The Supreme Master Ching Hai

The Supreme Master Ching Hai was born in Central Au Lac (Vietnam). At the age of eighteen, Master Ching Hai moved to England to study, and then later to France and then Germany, where She worked for the Red Cross and married a German physician. After two years of happy marriage, with Her husband's blessings, She left Her marriage in pursuit of enlightenment, thus fulfilling an ideal that had been with Her since Her childhood. This began a time of arduous pilgrimages to many different countries that ended only when She met a perfect living Master in the Himalayas. Master Ching Hai received the divine transmission of the inner Light and Sound, which She later called the Quan Yin Method. After a period of diligent practice, She attained Perfect Enlightenment.

To satisfy the longing of sincere Truth seekers, the Supreme Master Ching Hai offers the Quan Yin Method of meditation to people of all nationalities, religions and cultural backgrounds. Her message of love and peace brings spiritual liberation and hope to people throughout the world, reminding all to uphold Truth, Virtue, and Beauty in life.

4 HERMIT *01*

5 GOODY *57*

6 BOYO *101*

7 LADY *137*

8 POMAS *159*

9 ZOLO *193*

10 HALLY *219*

In speaking of God or the Supreme Spirit, Master instructs us to use original non-sexist terms to avoid the argument about whether God is a She or a He.

She + He = Hes (as in Bless)
Her + Him = Hirm (as in Firm)
Hers + His = Hiers (as in Dear)

Example: When God wishes, Hes makes things happen according to Hiers will to suit Hirmself.

As a creator of artistic designs as well as a spiritual teacher, Supreme Master Ching Hai loves all expressions of inner beauty. It is for this reason that She refers to Vietnam as "Au Lac" and Taiwan as "Formosa." Au Lac is the ancient name of Vietnam and means "happiness." And the name Formosa, meaning "beautiful," reflects more completely the beauty of the island and its people. Master feels that using these names brings spiritual elevation and luck to the land and its inhabitants.

Nobody wanted this Australian Shepherd because he vomits often and eats a lot all the time. He was six months old when he was squeezed in a round cage that was too small for him to turn around! When I got him, he was shy and afraid of humans, but he's okay now. He's loving, loyal, protective, and sticky.

Nicknames: Food Processor, Heh Heh (panting often), Chip Ahoy (chocolate chip cookie color), Ruby Blue (eyes red in the spot light but blue in day time), The Hype.

He's always excited being around me, or people he knows. He would look into your eyes adoringly, lovingly while you're petting him, as if the whole world doesn't exist except you. You feel so loved, so special.

He's good with other dogs, but does not trust all humans. If he's with me, he accepts humans, but distances himself if approached. He'll shy behind me and not show any sign of socialization. But if he knows you are friends, or family, he will adore you like no others.

While loving to other dogs, if playing tug of war, he'll always win. He'll always catch the tennis ball first in the air or on the ground; even if Goody gets the ball or toys, he will extract from Goody's mouth – friendly-wise but persistently the winner!

He loves to sit at my feet, no matter how uncomfortable the ground, rather than go to a soft bed – Well! Most of my dogs are like that anyway – sticky –

If humans would devote themselves to God as thus, they'd sure attain Heaven!

Though I do look friendly.

Well, don't I?

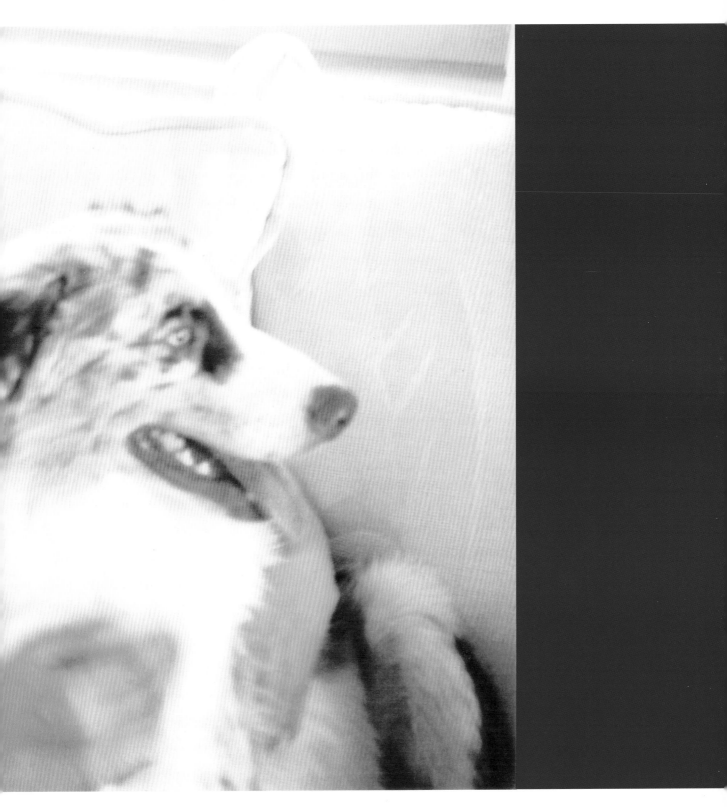

Actually,
I never thought
that I could be a sailor.

And swimming…

does tire you out!

Goody, did you hear some noise?

Ah-hah! They want us to row
them across!

That was a good "boating."

Which **famous model** dog

do I remind you of?

Well! I don't know either.
I just look like a model
Anyway.
"Methinks"

I think, I could have a glamorous career as a guard, or

acting as a lion

or, as a ghost!

Oh, well!
A lovely pet, anyone?

Maybe…just maybe…

I have been a tiger, last life!

…or maybe…a wuf.

No...a wolf!

Is there life
after death?
Why am I here?

Is it possible to keep my folks
for many many lives?
(I love them so much!)
I don't want to lose them.

Who can give me the answers
for all the past and future?

I try to sit, in quiet meditation.
But my heart wanders
in all directions!

Nothing is better than solitude!

I could stay here like… forever.

Master said: "Meditation can solve problems."
(Well! I don't have any! Away Mom took them.)

But, wait…
Which way
did I come from?

I think I am lost!...

It's getting dark quickly here in the forest.

Where am I?

Master! Mom!
Take me home!

What…on earth…is this?

OK, CHILL OUT!

Let's see…

It looks like sand,
but it doesn't feel like sand!
It sticks to your paws,
And freezes them all!

I feel…gooood though!
It is fresh and cold…

Exercise keeps you warm…
Heh, heh… keeps you too warm!

Hwoo! Hwoo… I had …
enough,…I…tell…you!

HOW should one actually meditate
on the snow?

I think I'll just try...

They say the cold keeps you awake during meditation

It's cold alright.

But I'm kinda dozing off.

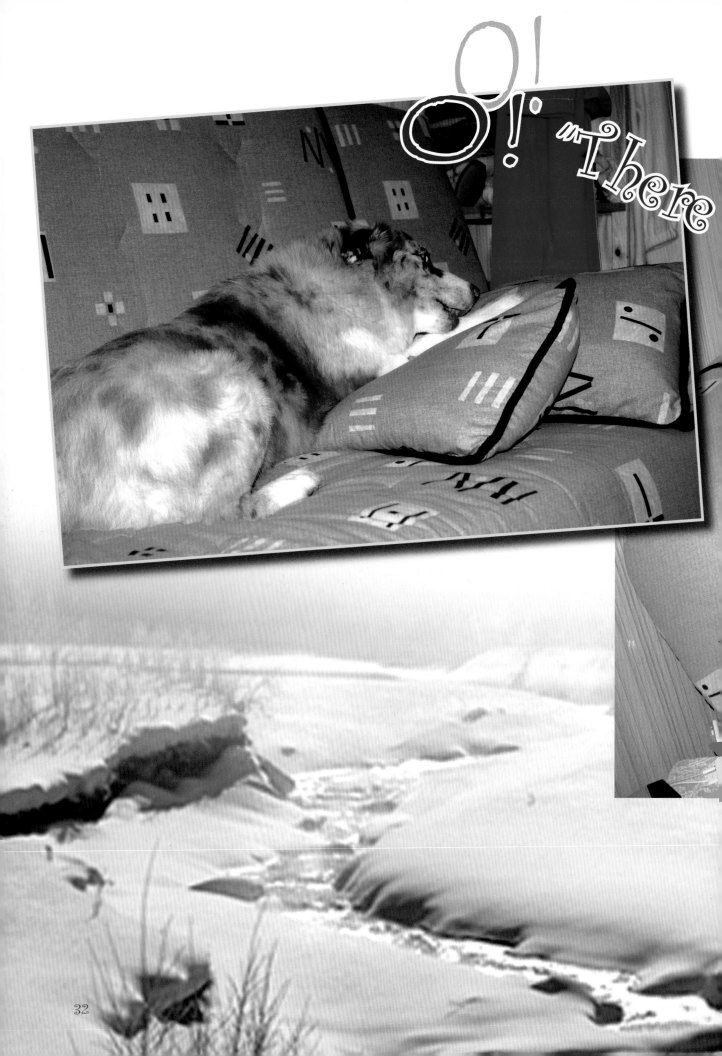

O! "There

"o place like home"

It's not just a home,
It's my Heaven!

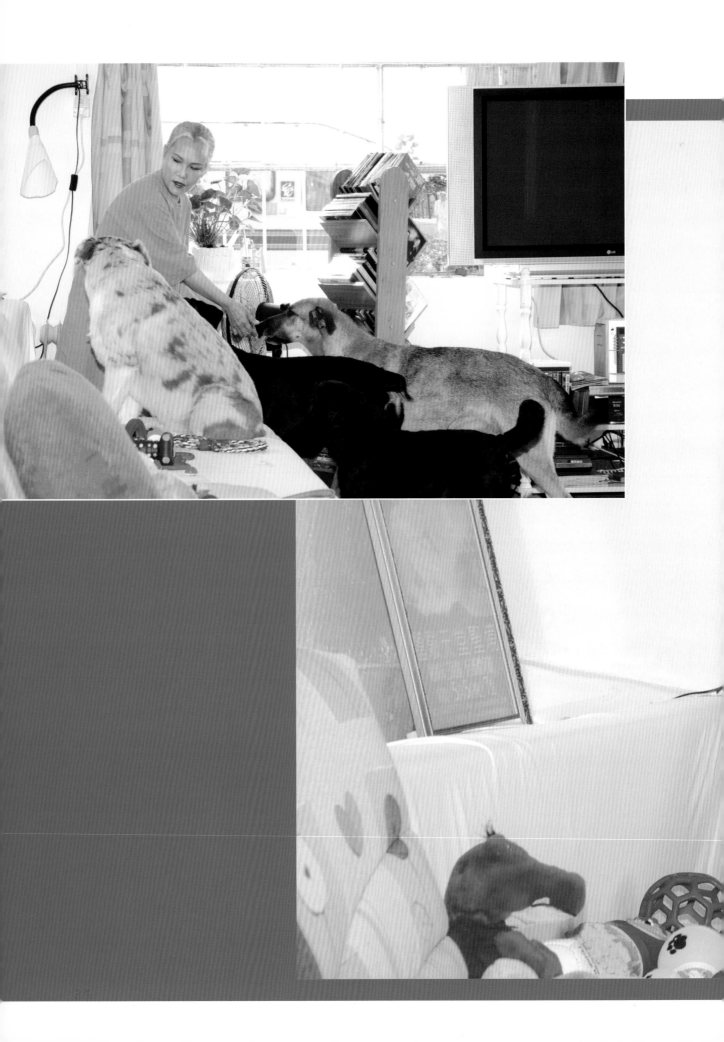

Can you find the 4 differences between
these two Shepherds in the photos?

If yes, reward yourself with a
similar one, from the dog shelter.

I am tempted to taste some of these
while they are all busy.

GUESS

who is eating what?

We took it from the vegetable basket in the kitchen, always! No one ever said anything!

(ANSWER: Next page)

Now I munch the raw potato!

Ah-ha! Caught me "red-handed"!
But the potato's gone. No more
evidence (eaten by me & Lucky)

But the carrot.
Well!...This is the 3rd one.

Hey! Camera!

Haven't you seen a blue-eyed Australian Shepherd before?

Heh!Heh!Heh.

You run alone, Goody. I'll just take a pause.

42

It's tricky, the staircase!
Whoever made this
had no dogs in mind!

But if "Mom Mom" is up
there, I'll climb up.
—Well, can I really?

43

They too!

It's a little too crowded at lunch, no?

You're right. I need some space.

What is Happy drinking?

Let's find out in a blink!

time story...

is the best-time story

Z

Z

Z

Z

Z

Now, where could Mom sleep tonight???

"Mom, you are welcome
on 'my' bed!"
(Actually it's her bed)

"I think it's better I go!..

...and be comfortable on the floor. Thank you!"

GOODY

He was cooped up in a small square cage, couldn't move, bony, had to eat his own poop — Ready to be thrown out — without feeding! Very sick when he first came, in-house quarantined 2 months. OK, now — Loves shadows 24/7. He is loving, loyal, protective and sticky. Loves to be "hugged," will "bully" you to pet him when he needs one! If not getting the pet he wants, he will stay waiting on or under your lap "forever."

Nick names: Shadow Hunter, The Samurai, The Psychic, Drooley (will not beg for food, just drool from afar)

He is a gentleman with family members, never "barks back" at "big brother" Benny, always lets Hermit take whatever he wants from him — even from his mouth — and does not compete with any for food or toys. But he always welcomes whoever from the human family with some offering, even if that means your own slipper, your pillow, your phone or remote controller, full of his personal drool of affection. Being too sensitive, he detects people's energy and reacts accordingly, not always flattering to that person. Maybe all Rotweillers are similar. But he is a darling to love and be loved. He'd not bother you, just quietly plays with his own shadow or the tree's. Growling alone with his toys, and wanting some love now and then from you – and he persists till he gets it!

But he will shy away if you really do not want him near at times.

He is a macho type, but a sweet one!

We are definitely no racists!
We are the best buddies
that ever exist.

Can you guess my
favorite pastime?
(Hint: something to do
with a flashlight)

Right! Shadow-hunting!
Am a shadow-hunter!

Reward yourself by hugging
your dogs and get kisses from them.

If you don't have a dog,
And could afford one to adopt,
go ahead and be my hero!
Bravo!

I AM A
SHADOW HUNTER

Pose!
Ready!
Catch!

INSIDE OUT

?

Where does the shadow go?

64

We are...

Good buddies!

Love is looking in the same direction!

"In such beauty of nature,
all you fix to is shadows!"

"Leave
me alone
in ...
shadow!"

Lots of shadow under the trees

But it takes a toll on me!
Why does it have to be summer?
The heat seems to stay forever!

Chasing shadows
can be tiring.

It's nice to stay
by your side:

A loving!

65

Could I
watch out while
you nap?

Well,
of course,
buddy dearest!

Master said that "sharing is a good virtue."

Guess why I have such a perfect smile?

Answer:
I brush my teeth
every day. Honest!

Shadow, anyone?

I luv shadows
in the house.

I luv freedom when I'm out
walking leisurely.
Nicey!

But
where do I come from
and
whereto will I go???

For now, I go where she does.

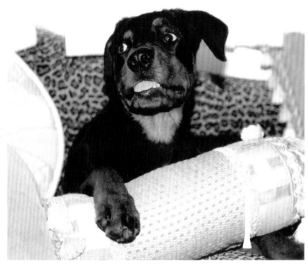

1

What does it mean: "smile"?

like...this?

2

3

Or...like...this?

OK! OK!
I got it—
smile big.

4

I look scary, don't I? (That photographer!)

OK! I hide those fangs. ♥

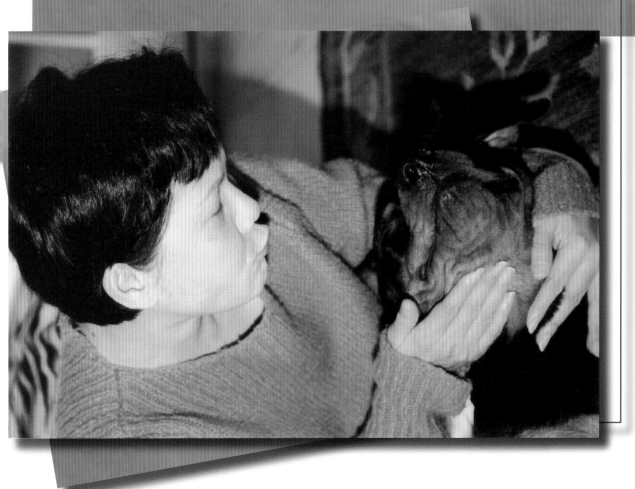

Forget it—the "cheese" stuff.
I am not showing my teeth this time
You made my photo look scary last shot.
I hate it a lot!

Are you done with photographing?
A puppy just wanna relax and "cooling."

This tree is alive.
That tree is dead.
What an ephemeral scene
I got in between!
How I long for something
that really lasts!

Hermit buddy,
        could you wag your head here and there?
                I wanna play with your shadow, OK Her?

Sometimes, one feels as if one is all alone.

It's nice

to have
someone:
A true
friendship.
To hold and
to keep.

I am looking for a hidden, cool corner.

I think
here is good!
For chasing shadows.

I think I'm "safe"!
No one knows where to find me,
and make me "walk the grass" today.

They "found" me.
And here I am!
Back home again.

It's not just the "greenie bone"
It's the l♥ve that goes with it!
I am sure, Ma'am, that's what it is!

"OK! OK! You won!
I am cornered!"

A green bone
For her freedom
And for me…yum
yum…

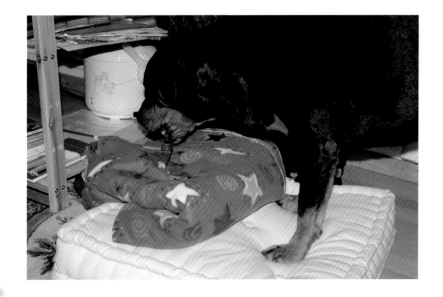

Just one more
green bone
I'll behave!
Please, Mom!

Ain't I cute?

What think you?
Should I?

87

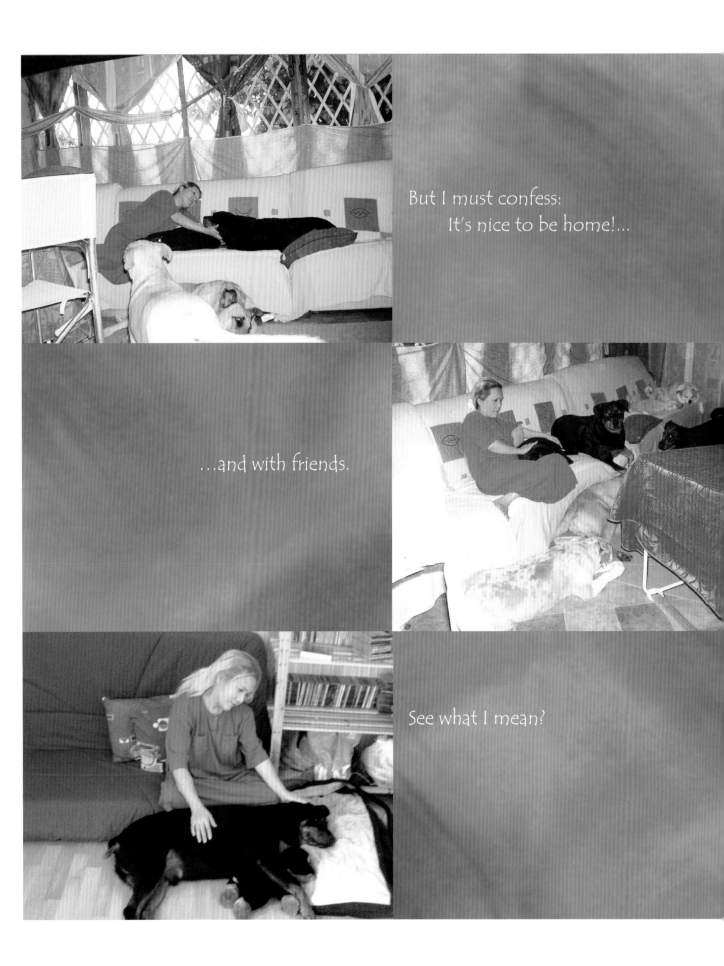

But I must confess:
    It's nice to be home!...

...and with friends.

See what I mean?

I am lonely…

…no more!

…and a sofa does good to the soul!
Furthermore…

…I don't understand why I should go
and stay in the Himalayas!…

And with my best friend.

Ah, but it's worth
the effort.

Am I a little too heavy
or what?

It's too high.
Wish I had a ladder.

How do I catch
this haughty shadow?

Mom's scent

when Mom's not home. At least.

It's all an illusion,
but it's sure cold!
Now what! It snows…
Already?
Geez!

What weather!
　　Sun and snow at the same time!
　　　　Confusing this shadow of mine.

One feels weird
just to stand here.

I am sinking, even!
It's not 'quicksnow', is it?

I should think fast!

Now, what would
Master do in this
situation?

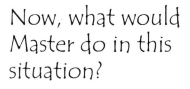

I'd better get going.

But where
should I go?
Everywhere is
but snow!

I don't know how the yogis could meditate in the Himalayas!!!
Some even wear nothing. Master said they're called "Naga"
But if I stay longer here
I may turn into "Nada"!

I still think that a warm jacket
won't hurt any yogis…
especially me!…

BOYO

Boyo (BoBo) is from Hungary. In the beginning, he was cool, reserved, and scared. He likes the corner and is afraid of thunder. He immediately came to kiss me the first time he saw me. He's doing well presently. He loves to sleep in my room (well, they all do). He is now more well-built. At first, he looked a little weird, as if his head was "swimming" over his body (too skinny and unproportionate). His pale-colored coat could be seen through to the skin (and that was in the winter, when temperatures could be -30°C).

He's okay now. He is loving, loyal, protective, and sticky!

Boyo is so loving and appreciative – but still afraid of thunder. Every time it strikes, he runs to my room to hide and will not eat for that day, no matter what food, or his favorite! I can't imagine what he must have been feeling before without shelter!

He loves to lay as near as possible to my side, even if that means forsaking his sofa, bed or comfy blanket. He is a real gentleman, often letting his friend Lady have her fill first, or letting her eat his share as well even if it's a fav. green bone.

Usually he is polite, quiet and affectionate absolutely to humans. But, he can flex his skinny muscles to restore order if any new dog in the house makes too much commotion.

"Before"

I am Boyo (affectionately called "Bo" or
  "BoBo" by my Mom). I looked something
like this before (I don't really recall exactly
how I looked). I just remember the cold shed,
the chain, the same frozen food every day.
The thin hair that hardly covered my skin;
the head that was protruding and seemed
to be bigger & separated from my thin body;
The dirt hole that couldn't keep me from
the rain, wind, snow, and the temperature of
minus 30° below zero...

"After"

I LOOK LIKE THIS NOW.

My hair grew thicker, gained more luster.
My whole body became perfectly proportionate.
My heart became perfectly happy…
My soul became elevated.
And I love life.

How about a...cool...

"breakfast in bed"?

When one doesn't feel too well with thunder outside!

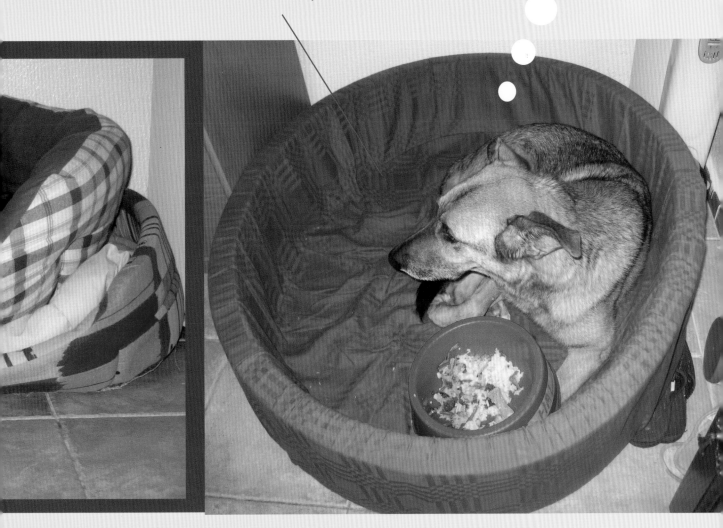

This is my human friend

and my 𝓛𝓸𝓿𝓮!

This is my garden (shared, but mine).

And my buddy, black but kind!

Don't you just

ove this weather?

But…
I'm not used to
being outside
anymore.

Can't believe I survived Hungarian outdoor winters
with only the sky
for a roof all that time!

I forgot
what snow looks like,
what frozen ice
feels like…

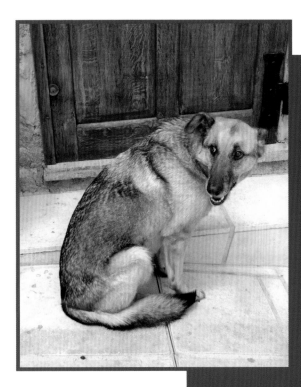

I don't like it outside.
Not too long.

I love my home.
I love my sofa.

You can see why!

115

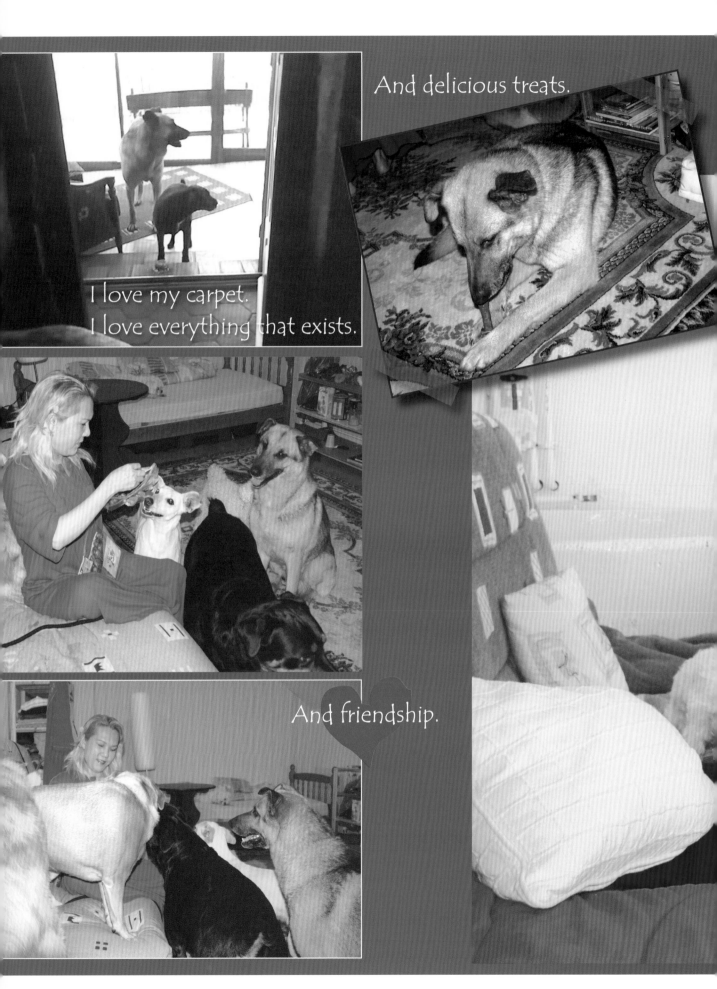

And delicious treats.

I love my carpet.
I love everything that exists.

And friendship.

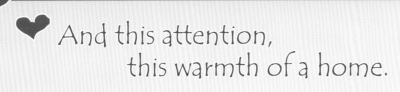

And this attention,
this warmth of a home.

Don't be fooled. I am not lonely.

Especially when it
rains and Lightenings
and thunders!
I am scared and
traumatized by
bad weather.
I am sensitive!
No one ever knows.
(But Mom cares for Boyo!)

Still, I don't like
being too long
outside.

Home!
Here, it's Heaven.

This is my home

And by now
you surely know
to be loved
is the best thing in the world.

PomPom!
Would it be possible
that you can't finish the green bone?

124

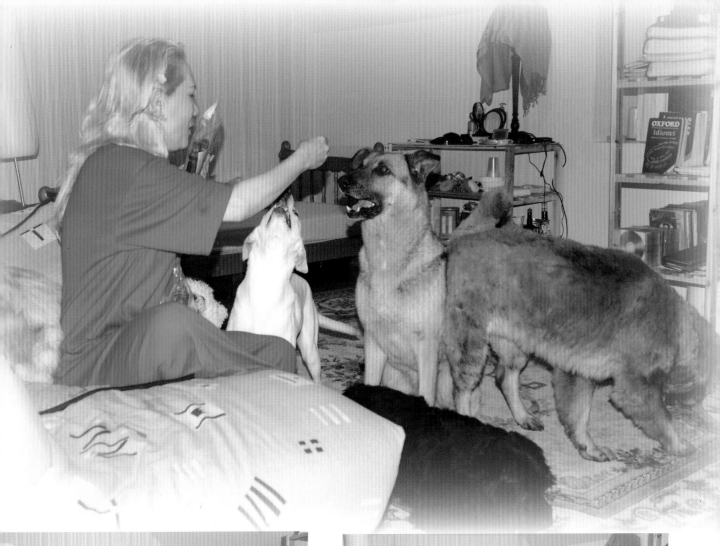

...just asking! So...

I knew you'd say no.

Meditate?
We do it our way!

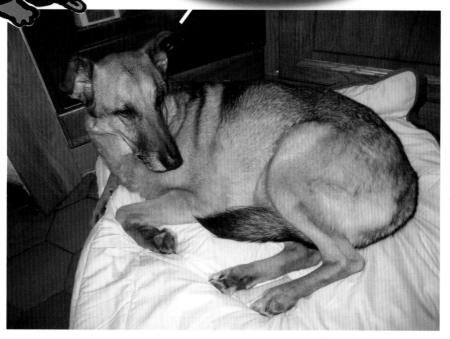

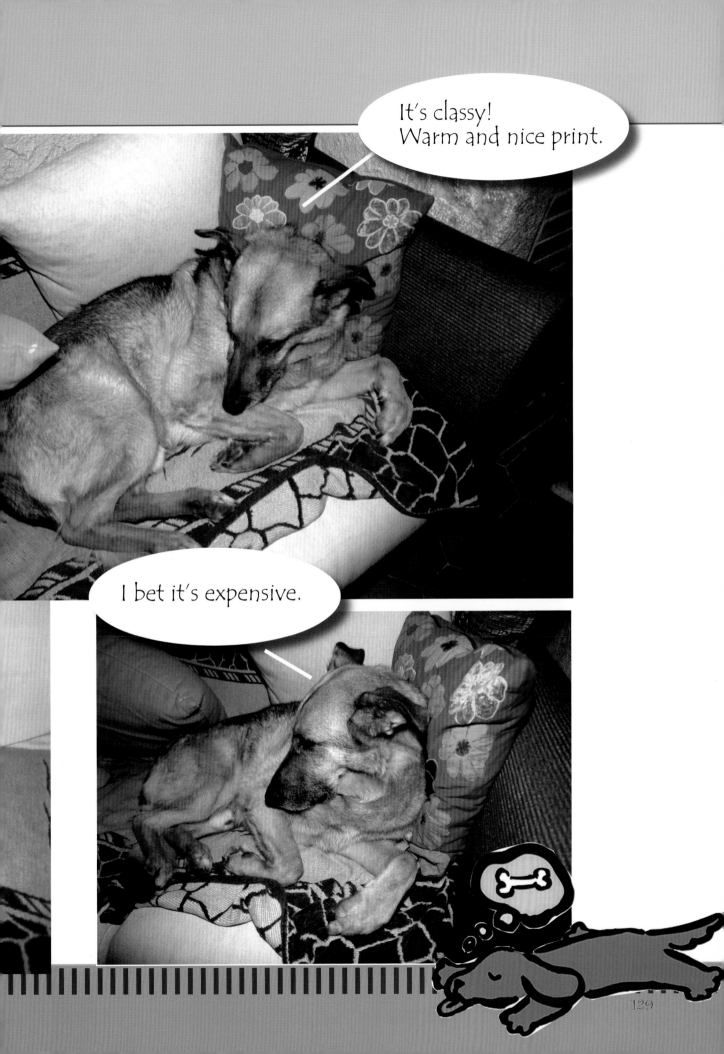

129

But Mom said
it's better to
meditate on
the floor

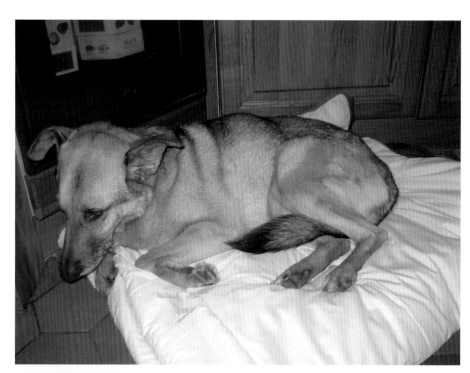

so one will
not fall
too far
in case…
(you know!)

Never had this quilt
in my life
before!

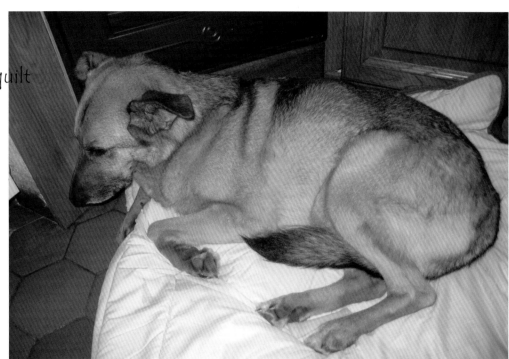

It's the color of snow.
But how warm it is!
I do actually
appreciate it.
Thanks, Mom!

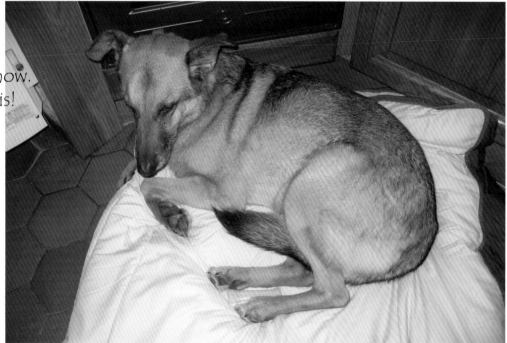

Still, I wonder
if anyone ever
became a Buddha
sitting on a sofa?

I like hiding sometimes.
From thunder from the sky.
Oh, how I used to be frightened
with nowhere to hide!

But I let Happy (sometimes)
have my
secret
hideout
(on loan).

And we do have a real fireplace
lit up in winter.
We sit around together.
O! Heaven on Earth!

LADY

Lady is a strong, affectionate bully! She is from Hungary, where she was filthy, with hair all twisted and matted. She is okay now. She's loving, loyal, protective, and sticky.

When we first met, I told Lady to sit. But she ignored the request and went away.

But since we sleep together in the same trailer, she has become more cooperative. Now every time she sees me, without command, she will just sit quietly and wait for me to pet her or give her treat and the "Good Girl" comment!

No matter how chaotic the dogs or how noisy they are around her, she just sits still and quietly, with the proud attitude of "Good Girl."

I just have to hug her each time. She's adorable, especially while doing that pose. Despite her toughness, she purrs like a kitten when I pet her, all four up or not, and very respectful to my requests now. I love this girl. Call her my Princess, my Cookie, my Choco (her chocolate color). She is such a love!

She has become so tamed, so mellow with each passing day. One cannot help but to love her so much!

I am Lady from Hungary.
Nice to meet you, Buddy!

Lady: Captain Cook-ky.
Lifts legs, humps like boys.
Fears nothing
and nobody!

She looks sweet,
But she's so tough.
Don't mess with her.
Stay away …better.

What!!...This is the best smile you can have
from me.
really!
I've never smiled
into the camera before!
I never smiled at all.

That is, until I met "Mom".
You remember how I was before, right?
Just to refresh your memory, turn to the next page.

I do not love the snow, especially in Hungary.
It was always cold in the winter (can be -30°C).

This was almost how I looked before,
except for the long, matted, smelly hair!
That never knew a barber.
And my left eye
is torn forever.
Every time Mom looks at it
She still feels a sharp "prick"!

141

I love indoors.

I love outdoors.

143

Inside

or out

Life is woof anyhow! ♥

It's like

Heaven

Tastes like Heaven (dog's).

146

Mom,
can I
have
more?

Sure, love
is better
than
anything.

Well, but…
Green-
bones are
good good!

Life is as
woof as
you...

...yourself
make it!
Methinks!

Quash! I can lift a leg as high
as you males too!

What they do, I can.

I am no short of any boy!

I, Lady, declare the control
of the male population here
starting with you!

Life is totally "cool."

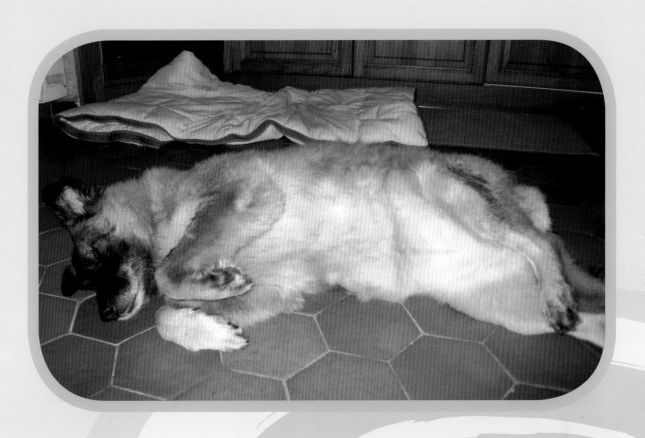

Cool…like clean indoors
and terra floor!

I love my treats.
I love my house.

I love my lady,
and she me!

I love my garden.
I love nature.

I love all this.
Who wouldn't? And more…

I live happily ever after.

POMAS

Pomas came from Hungary. He was shy, reserved, and easily dominated by bigger dogs. But no more! He is strong and confident now. He will growl back at any-size bully.

He's loving, loyal, protective and sticky. If he wants a "hug," he'll come and quietly put his head on your lap!

Nicknames: PomPom, Genty, Sweet Boy.

Pomas is the most quiet of all my dogs and is a complete darling! He is a no-trouble, contented at all times, and gives only love to anyone he sees.

Now and then, when he sees the opportunity, he will quietly come to me and place his head gently on my lap for an affection "refill," leaving if other dogs come for the same.

Even though Boyo and he had some macho conflict before, he always shows love to Boyo by greeting him, rolling on his back or kissing the chap. And of course he adores humans. Any human is his friend – absolutely no question in his mind that a human is to be loved and revered! And his Motto: Live and let live.

Wonder how I did survive all those cold times!

I am Pomas (affectionately called "Pomy" or "PomPom" by Mom).

I look more handsome in real life. It's the photograph that makes me look sheepish! But...I looked worse before Mom took me in. I had dirty, matted hair and wet cold feet all day long in the winter.

So I often climbed on top of Boyo's shelter roof to keep dry for some moments. My open-door style doggie shed never made any difference in temperature, especially in the winter, when it could be minus 30° Celsius.

I told "Mom" when she was visiting and she tried to build a better place for me. They all wanted to help build it. But I was still feeling cold all day and more so at night.

Wonder how I did survive all those cold times! I just swooned out at night when it was too cold. And even worse, before that I was on a chain all the time. The next group of people were much nicer. They freed me so I could move around.

But the winter cold is still severe in Hungary. I just hung on!

First they told Mom that "we dogs are used to the cold." But the fact was that we had no choice.

We would know the difference if asked. After a few days, Mom couldn't bear it, so she took me and two others into her place, a small trailer used as her temporary abode.

It was a palace to us: there was a warm
heater, new fuzzy beds, temperate clean
water, and we got to sleep next to her small
bed. She asked her attendants to clean
us with vinegar water solution and damp
towels, and carry us into her place. She
greeted us with such warm welcome—
we felt loved! We wanted to stay forever.
She gave us the first warm meal ever in our
entire lives!

Every night, after her work, she got us in and shared her meals with us, or toasted thick slices of bread and melted butter on them! Our hearts also melted every time. Nothing had ever tasted so good as buttered toast in frozen winter nights!

Then she took us all with her wherever she went. The treatment just gets better. Life just gets nicer!...

And I am forever happy. The scars
on my body had been there long
before I even remember.

They just showed when I had been
bathed and given a haircut. When
Mom saw it the first time, she
cried and hugged me tight.

But I said she shouldn't worry.
The scar in my heart is healed already!
I love to be her dog.
I am the happiest doggie! 🩶

He conveyed the message that Mom is a great Master

She had five dogs before we met, but I don't mind. There is enough love for everyone. Besides, I get along well with all of them, especially Goody the Rottweiler. He is very enlightened and has taught me lots of things. We communicated even before we met. He conveyed the message that Mom is a great Master and that we should show respect; she is very good to animals and we were lucky to be with her, for he missed her much but couldn't see her just yet. He and four others were "counting the days to reunite with her soon."

So the next morning, we all gathered outside her trailer in a line to greet her. She was very happy to know the message as well as to see us, and rewarded us with some nice snacks from her plates!

I'll never forget those first days and nights with her. It seems still like yesterday! We all love "Mom" very much! And forever.

Now, I and my friends are happily living with her and the other dogs. We have good, warm food every day, especially prepared for us. We have vitamins, snacks, warm beds, soft, clean sofas, and a nice garden to walk around. Life can't be any better. Thank heavens for all we have and enjoy. I wish other dogs in the world can be in a similar situation, like ours, enjoying love and happiness.

If she

I'd better watch my weight!

keeps feeding us!

Just "shopping" round the corner, no?!

Exercise does you good—
keeps you fit and trim!

No worry, I'll be back
with some nylon bones!

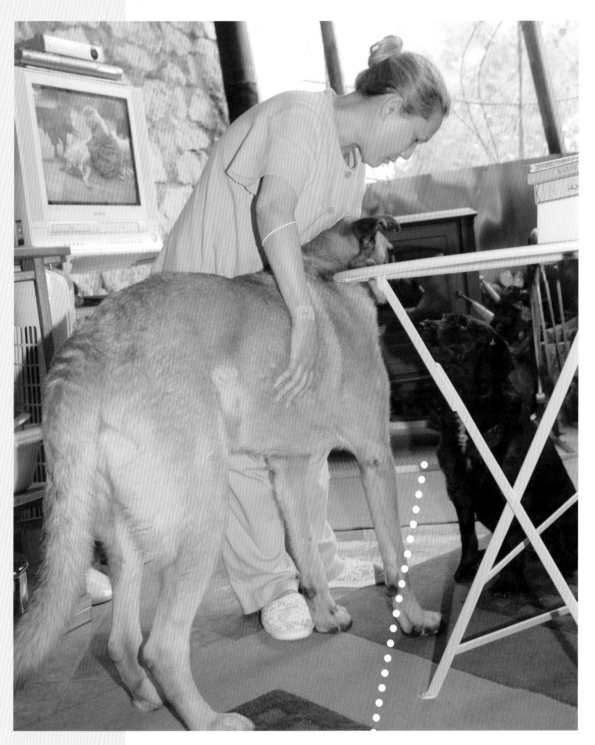

Okay, my horse!
Did you say "Coaler"?
He is bigger alright,
But I am blacker!
Certainly not afraid of your type!...
Do you want to try…
….outside?

And now, who is taller?

Let's see who chews faster, "snowflake"!

Though I call him snowflake, white rice, paley...

But we are buddies.

No racism ever by us doggies!

Same with this guy.
I call him biggy,
he calls me darky.
But we are totally
Okay!

And life is a dog's paradise.
We eat, we sleep, we play
under her care and protective eyes.

And we can stay forever
with her,
thank God.
Here, we are loved,
we are warm, we are a herd,
a bunch of spoiled
buddy dogs!

I'm listening.

But I doubt it if you have a better story

than what I've been telling.

ZOLO

He was left in the open, chained day and night, in Hungary, in rain, snow, or shine. After I bought him from the ex-owner, he had to be treated for three months for exterior wounds (from the tight chain on the neck) and internal illness. He is okay now. He's loving, loyal, protective and sticky.

He's so used to the indoors and company now, if left alone outside he crys.

Nicknames: The Horse, Biggie body.

Zolo is trying his best to be a tamed family dog, even though he was treated unkindly before and thus distrusted humans.

Even then, when we first met, he came to kiss me and gave his paw as sign of friendship, despite his terrible condition at that time! That was a horrible environment that he was in – dog poops piled up next to him like a small hill! He had a loaf of filthy hard, half-eaten bread, a concrete yard floor and no water in sight. He was covered with dirt, thin falling hair and a sharp, a tight collar, and a chain around his neck that cut into his skin, which our vets had to perform surgery to heal after we took him with us.

He was left there to guard an empty house, dead or alive with flies, insects buzzing around and on him day or night!

When he first entered my house, he would bark, jump at and attack repeatedly any new human. But after a period of training, he is very gentle now, and shows affection to all in my house. But as any big dog, one should have a healthy caution; even if the dog has no intention to do harm, his strength could accidentally hurt you!

Despite his toughness, he is very cooperative now and so patient with Hally the Toppy who has a strange sense of affection for him (Translation: Controlling Jump-on, Catch-up and Yell-down Bully Act)

He is so affectionate, it's amazing, especially for a dog who has known no love before. Every time after an outing with other people, he comes running in to find me for a snuggle and will not leave till I tell him to, and even then, sticks as close as possible. Though there are people in my place who help with feeding and caring for him, he knows who loves him the most. His sense of loyalty is absolute, and he shows his love anytime.

I am Zolo.

Came from Hungary Winter
To the Mediterranean Summer.

From chained to free.

Now, life is as perfect as it could be!

Is life
always as black and white?

No, life is a paradise.

Life is **SUNSHINE.**

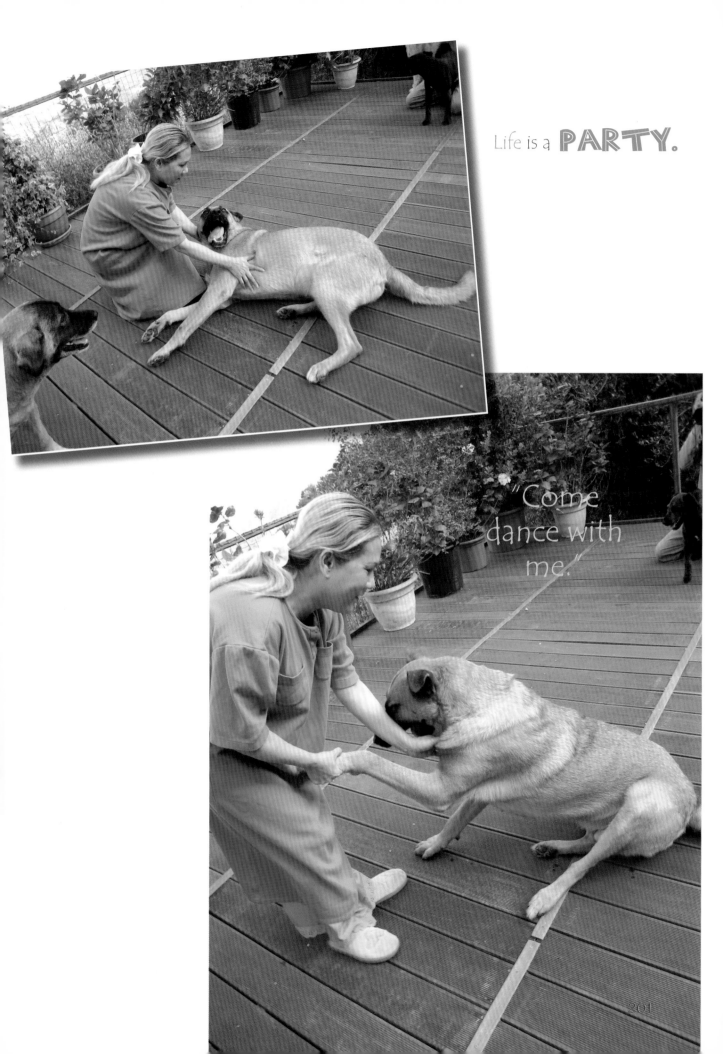

Life is a **PARTY.**

"Come
dance with
me."

And, it's possible…

to **love** humans.

And this is the woman
who makes life different.

Long live
freedom.

Long live
my human!

Long live friendship.

We are big, we are tiny.
But we're good-size buddies.

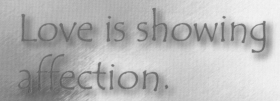

Love is showing affection.

Love is also

sharing

the same

aspiration.

We need to talk.

OK, OK!
You are the top!

Yeh! You always do, toppy.

"I want a ride!"

WATCHING OVER YOU ♥

♥ Sleep nice.

♥ I'll watch over you,

♥ dear Puh-puh.

I love my
new home!
(first ever.)

"Come on, guys! Do some exercise!"

I love this pack and the pack leader.
Clap your hands if you know who!

She's full of
"treats"

and full of
wonders.

...And the stories she tells

We'd like to listen forever.

This is my home

where I feel loved and safe

where we share life and love forever!
I thank Heaven and her!

HALLY

A chained watchdog from Hungary, Hally was Zolo's neighbor. There was another dog of Hally's size, but because it was too cold he died. Hally is tough and bullying, but now sweet to humans. He can jump very high, even through windows and gate! He's a self-proclaimed top dog and acts like one, but is absolutely harmless to humans. He doesn't get on well with fellow mate, Zolo, although they're from the same background. He's loving, loyal, protective, and sticky!

Nicknames: Russian Roulet (Russian name Jumpalot), Jumpy Jerky, The Acrobat, The Gym (All 4 are the same meaning), Toppy (Likes to climb on top of other dogs), Beary (Looks like a bear)

Actually, Hally just wants to help in retaining order in the house.

He wants to protect humans from Zolo, fearing his guard dog habit which might turn to aggression. He wants to teach Zolo friendliness to people, at even his own risk!

Hally is an absolute human's friend - incredible for a dog who was chained day and night, winter and summer, in a desolate farm yard as he was.

He adores the human world, turning his belly anytime one is near for a rub, or putting his front paws on you to hug you in his "cute" way. One cannot resist but to love him dearly.

Even though he seems to bully Zolo, he loves him much. He likes to lie next to Zolo, throwing his whole weight sideways repeatedly to greet Zolo after each "separation" (meaning he came in a few seconds before Zolo did after an outing and is waiting to be cleaned before re-entering the house).

It's me,

Hally

the top dog

from Hungary,

survivor of the two

through harsh winter,

hot summer

without a hole

to turn to!

It's nice to be
free at long last.

I had bad mood.
If you had been chained
in the freezing winter
and burning summer,
never knew warmth, care, or love
or the likes for so long,
wouldn't you be bad too?

But I can be "friendly."

223

I'm still The Guard!

*As I was
trained to be!
(just kidding)
who would be
so silly
to do that job...
Woaf!*

I'm actually friendly.

No??

Look!
I'm smiling
(well, that's my style).

I also want "pet pet"...

There! There! This is what I'm talking about!

*I never
had this
love before.*

And this hug! Oh!

GOD!
I FEEL
LOVED!

I follow only this guide

all the rest of my life. 🐾

Outside

Nice
and sunny

ZzZ
Inside

Soft
and
comfy!

229

And lots
of buddies!

And lots
of toys,

and lots
of treats!
Oooh wee!

It will be 🐾

My turn now! 🐾🐾

Did anyone become "Buddha"
sitting under an olive tree?

(I think, I feel that's possible)

Or while

rolling

the floor

(I feel I'm already in Buddha's land, yo!!)

What's "up"?

Maybe I was a bear in a former life.

Feel like I am a big bear.

*I remember somehow
climbing trees
somewhere
in some lives!*

*Should I try to climb?
"Now"?*

Why! I've been to the gym lately.

Acrobat, any body?

Sorry I called you Jumpy Jerky!

Can we...like

shake paws,

peace?...

— "Maybe" —

Say it, buddy,

I am

the Alpha!!

Size?

Doesn't matter!

LOVE THY NEIGHBOR'S DOG

Love Thy Neighbor's Dog

Bella is getting new winter shirt, newly hand- sewn socks (by Mom)
and a new diet (Ha, Veggie! It's good for me.)

EPILOGUE

The book can only describe a fraction of what an extraordinary being a dog can be - only dog keepers know about it.

Each dog merits a whole big book to detail all his life and characters. But, all in all, dogs are a very noble race of beings.

I hope to let the readers enjoy some glimpse of the beautiful ways that dogs walk the Earth with us, and through them, understand more about other beings.

I want you to know that, we (all souls) choose to incarnate in the physical realm through a variety of forms. But all beings are like us. They are born to live out their time, to contribute to a colorful life on this planet. It thus behooves us to be their good co-inhabitants, with all due respect, peace and love.

If, in our lifetime, we chance to have a personal relationship with anyone in the animal kingdom, consider ourselves blessed and lucky!

Master *thanks* the following individual for their meticulous assistance:

Crystal Vo, Victor Ngo, T. June, Thomas Lux, Steven André, Danny Vu *(Cameramen)*

Annie Yu, Nadir Yen, Chien Wei Ba-Li, Kim Cheng, Jackie *(Design and Layout)*

Gary Lai, Nadir Yen, Yu Hui-Chun, Wang Bor Tang, Sofia, Jackie *(Graphic Design)*

Lynn McGee, Jane Chu, Wenqing Li, Becky Chen, Sun Wang,
Clair, Moon *(Copy Proofreading)*

*"...And for permeating
your work with love"*

~ Supreme Master Ching Hai

245

To improve the lives of all sentient beings, including that of animals…

🐾 Healthy, Cozy Doghouses

Our merciful Supreme Master Ching Hai is constantly thinking of ways to improve the lives of all sentient beings, including that of animals. Under Her careful instructions, a series of comfortable doghouses were designed to ensure warm, cozy homes for human's best friend. Each state-of-the-art doghouse boasts the following features: a non-toxic solid wood structure with offset doors for protection from wind and rain, a spacious porch covered with plexiglass sheeting material, cushioned medical-grade foam flooring for comfort, and removable windows for more air circulation in summer. The homes are also easy to assemble and to clean.

Even with such luxurious abodes for our canine friends, Master Ching Hai reminds "owners" to be sure to bring pets indoors during times of extreme heat or cold, or at night if living in dangerous zones, so the dogs will not become prey for wild animals or thieves. Actually, the dog house should be only for play and day-time, if necessary or if desired: Dogs are better inside the "owner's" house.

(For more details, please check our Website: http://www.godsdirectcontact.org.tw/eng/news/163/index2.htm, Holistic Animal Care section)

Happy Doggie-Celestial Clothes and Sleeping Mattresses for Dogs

Also per Master Ching Hai's compassionate instructions, the first-ever series of Happy Doggie Celestial Clothes and Sleeping Mattresses have been designed. These include a wide range of styles to meet the needs of dogs of all sizes. The doggie clothes are attractive in appearance and practical in their protective warmth, allowing human's loyal friends to look smart and stay warm in cold weather.

(For more details, please check our Website: http://www.godsdirectcontact.org.tw/eng/news/167/index2.htm , Holistic Animal Care section)

Food for a Healthy Doggie

Under Master Ching Hai's caring guidance, a healthy, natural and balanced vegetarian dog food was developed for our canine companions. This product is completely free of animal products and has been exclusively formulated by nutritionists. With main ingredients that include soy protein isolate, corn, oats and other grains, this wholesome and balanced diet is easy to digest and metabolize. It improves the dog's oral health and immune system and gives a glossy coat of hair, not to mention high energy levels.

Ever so thoughtful, Master Ching Hai suggests that it is better to feed freshly-prepared food to the dogs, and that ready food can be kept as an alternative when no fresh food is available or on busy days.

(For more details, please check our Website: http://www.godsdirectcontact.org.tw/eng/news/175/index.htm)

Related Information

For more information about communicating with and caring for our animal friends, along with inspiring stories from Master about Her other special animal companions, please refer to the following videotapes and DVDs.

DVD 712 The Divine Intelligence of Animals
20010605 Florida Center, U.S.A.

#714 Dogs Are Wonderful Beings
20010606 Florida Center, U.S.A.

DVD 718 Love is always good
20010607 Florida Center, U.S.A.

DVD 716 A Natural Way to Love God
20010608 Florida Center, U.S.A.

#738 Simple Living (Master & Residents)
20010426, 20010501, 20010512, 20010521 Florida Center, U.S.A.

DVD 711 The Hotel Called Life
20010623 Fresno, California, U.S.A.

#717 The Virtues Of a Good Neighbor
20010611 Florida Center, U.S.A.

#730 To Communicate by Love
20011225, 20011226 Florida Center, U.S.A.

#733 To Live with Noble Purpose
20010610 Florida Center, U.S.A.

#734 The Touch of a Master
20011226~20011227 Florida Center, U.S.A.

#740 Learning to Live in Harmony: Master's Birthday Celebration 2002
20020511 Florida Center, U.S.A.

DVD 719 Overcoming Bad Habits
20010609 Florida Center, U.S.A.

#724 Sincerity and Purity of Heart
20010612~20010616 Florida Center, U.S.A.

DVD 728 The Blessing of a Loving Thought
20011226 Florida Center, U.S.A.

#735 The Courage to Change
20011228~20011230 Florida Center, U.S.A.

DVD 755 The Laughing Saints
20030203 Florida Center, U.S.A.

DVD 756 The Value of Being Honest
20030216, 20030218 Florida Center, U.S.A.

DVD 771 A Youth's Passion
20060612

DVD 772 Laughing Through Life
20060615

DVD 773 Unconditional Devotion
20060612~20060707

DVD 780 The Dogs and the Birds in My Life

The Spiritual Teachings by The Supreme Master Ching Hai

The Key of Immediate Enlightenment

A collection of The Supreme Master Ching Hai's lectures. Available in Aulacese (1-15), Chinese (1-10), English (1-5), French (1), Finnish (1), German (1-2), Hungarian (1), Indonesian (1-5), Japanese (1-4), Korean (1-11), Mongolian (1,6), Portuguese (1-2), Polish (1-2), Spanish (1-3), Swedish (1), Thai (1-6), and Tibetan (1).

The Key of Immediate Enlightenment – Questions and Answers

A collection of questions and answers from Master's lectures.
Available in Aulacese (1-4), Bulgarian, Chinese (1-3), Czech, English (1-2), French, German, Hungarian, Indonesian (1-3), Japanese, Korean (1-4), Portuguese, Polish, and Russian.

The Key of Immediate Enlightenment – Special Edition/Seven-Day Retreat

A collection of Master's lectures in 1992 during a Seven-Day Retreat in San Di Mun, Formosa.
Available in English and Aulacese.

The Key of Immediate Enlightenment – Special Edition/1993 World Lecture Tour

A six-volume collection of The Supreme Master Ching Hai's lectures during the 1993 World Lecture Tour. Available in English and Chinese.

Letters Between Master and Spiritual Practitioners

Available in Aulacese (1-2), Chinese (1-3), English (1), Spanish (1)

Master Tells Stories

Available in Aulacese, Chinese, English, Japanese, Korean, Spanish, and Thai.

Of God and Humans – Insights from Bible Stories

Available in English and Chinese.

God Takes Care of Everything –
Illustrated Tales of Wisdom from The Supreme Master Ching Hai

Aulacese, Chinese, English, French, Japanese, and Korean.

The Supreme Master Ching Hai's Enlightening Humor – Your Halo Is Too Tight!

Available in Chinese and English.

Coloring Our Lives

A collection of quotes and spiritual teachings by Master. Available in Chinese and English.

Secrets to Effortless Spiritual Practice

Available in Chinese and English.

God's Direct Contact – The Way to Reach Peace

A collection of The Supreme Master Ching Hai's lectures during Her 1999 European Lecture Tour.
Available in English and Chinese.

I Have Come to Take You Home

Available in Arabic, Aulacese, Bulgarian, Czech, Chinese, English, French, German, Greek, Hungarian, Indonesian, Italian, Korean, Polish, Spanish, Turkish, Romanian, and Russian.

Living in the Golden Age series
The Realization of Health – Returning to the Natural and Righteous Way of Living

Collected excerpts from the lectures of Supreme Master Ching Hai.
Available in English and Chinese.

Aphorisms

Gems of eternal wisdom from Master.
Available in English/Chinese, Spanish/Portuguese, French/German, and Korean.

The Supreme Kitchen – International Vegetarian Cuisine

A collection of culinary delicacies from all parts of the world recommended by fellow practitioners.
Available in English/Chinese, Aulacese, and Japanese.

The Supreme Kitchen – Home Taste Selections

Recipes in a bilingual edition: English /Chinese.

One World... of Peace through Music

A collection of interviews and musical compositions from the 1998 benefit concert at the Shrine
Auditorium in Los Angeles, California.
Trilingual edition: English/Aulacese/Chinese.

S.M. Celestial Clothes

Available in bilingual edition: English/Chinese.

The Collection of Art Creations by The Supreme Master Ching Hai – Painting Series

Through the painting of an artist, the artist's inner Self is revealed. You will be deeply touched by the
intense affection, childlike innocence and motherly love of the liberated One.
Available in English and Chinese.

The Dogs in My Life (1-2)

This two-volume book set of 500 pages is a fabulous real-life set of doggy tales published by Master
about Her canine companions.
Available in English and Chinese.

The Birds in My Life

In this beautifully illustrated picture-story book, Master Ching Hai shows us the secret to unlocking
the animals' inner world.
Available in English and Chinese.

The Noble Wilds

The third book written *by*
Supreme Master Ching Hai

Is coming soon!

Poetry Collections by The Supreme Master Ching Hai

Wu Tzu Poems
Available in Aulacese, Chinese and English.

Silent Tears
Available in English/German/French, English/Chinese, Aulacese, Spanish, Portuguese, Korean and Filipino.

The Dream of a Butterfly
Available in Aulacese, Chinese and English.

The Old Time
Available in Aulacese and English.

Pebbles and Gold
Available in Aulacese, Chinese and English.

The Lost Memories
Available in Aulacese, Chinese and English.

Traces of Previous Lives
Available in Aulacese, English and Chinese.

Traces of Previous Lives 1, 2, 3 (CD, Video, Audio tapes) Aulacese

A Path to Love Legends 1, 2, 3 (CD, Video, Audio tapes) Aulacese

Beyond the Realm of Time (CD, DVD) Aulacese

A Touch of Fragrance (CD) Aulacese

That and This Day (CD) Aulacese

Dream in the Night (CD, DVD) Aulacese

What the Hell! (CD) Aulacese

Please Keep Forever (CD) Aulacese

Songs & Compositions of The Supreme Master Ching Hai
(CD, DVD) English, Aulacese, Chinese

Song of Love
Supreme Master Ching Hai sings timeless songs in English and Aulacese
(CD, DVD) English, Aulacese

Jeweled Verses
(CD, DVD)
Song performance and poetry recitation in Aulacese by Supreme Master Ching Hai, written by renowned Aulacese poets.

The Golden Lotus
(CD, DVD)
Aulacese poetic songs

Audio and Video Tapes

Audio tapes, DVDs, music concerts DVD, CDs, MP3s and video tapes of The Supreme Master Ching Hai's lectures and Music & Concert DVDs are available in Arabic, Armenian, Aulacese, Bulgarian, Cantonese, Cambodia, Chinese, Croatian, Czech, Danish, Dutch, English, Finnish, French, German, Greek, Hebrew, Hungarian, Indonesian, Italian, Japanese, Korean, Malay, Mongolian, Nepali, Norwegian, Mandarin, Polish, Portuguese, Persian, Russian, Romanian, Sinhalese, Slovenian, Spanish, Swedish, Thai, Turkish and Zulu. Catalog will be sent upon request. All direct inquiries are welcome.

Please visit our bookshop's website to download our catalogue and summaries of the contents of Master's latest publications:

http://www.smchbooks.com/ (in English and Chinese).

To order Master's publications,

please visit http://www.theCelestialShop.com to purchase online.

Or contact:

The Supreme Master Ching Hai International Association Publishing Co., Ltd., Taipei, Formosa

Tel: (886) 2-87873935 / Fax: (886) 2-87870873

E-mail: smchbooks@Godsdirectcontact.org

ROC Postal Remittance Account No.19259438 (for Formosa orders only)

Postal Account: : The Supreme Master Ching Hai International Association Publishing Co., Ltd.

Free Sample Booklet download

The Key of Immediate Enlightenment
(in 60 languages)
http://sb.godsdirectcontact.net/
http://www.direkter-kontakt-mit-gott.org/download/index.htm
http://www.Godsdirectcontact.org/sample/
http://www.Godsdirectcontact.us/com/sb/

How to Contact US

The Supreme Master Ching Hai International Association
P.O. Box 9, Hsihu Miaoli Hsien, Formosa (36899), R.O.C.
P.O.Box 730247, San Jose, CA 95173-0247, U.S.A.

Book Department

divine@Godsdirectcontact.org
Fax: 1-240-352-5613 / 886-949-883778
(You are welcome to join us in translating Master's books into other languages.)

The Supreme Master Ching Hai International Association Publishing Co., Ltd.

smchbooks@Godsdirectcontact.org
Tel: 886-2-87873935
Fax: 886-2-87870873
http://www.smchbooks.com

News Group

lovenews@Godsdirectcontact.org
Fax: 1-801-7409196 / 886-946-728475

Spiritual Information Desk

lovewish@Godsdirectcontact.org

Fax: 886-946-730699

A Journey through Aesthetic Realms TV Program Videotapes

TV@Godsdirectcontact.org

Fax: 1-413-751-0848 (USA)

S.M. Celestial Co., Ltd.

smcj@mail.sm-cj.com

Tel: 886-2-87910860

Fax: 886-2-87911216

http://www.sm-cj.com

Celestial Shop

http://www.theCelestialShop.com

http://www.edenrules.com

Quan Yin WWW Sites

God's direct contact—The Supreme Master Ching Hai International Association's global Internet:
http://www.Godsdirectcontact.org.tw/eng/links/links.htm

This portal provides a directory of links to Quan Yin Web sites in a variety of languages, as well as
24-hour access to the TV program *A Journey through Aesthetic Realms*. You may also download
multilingual editions of *The Key of Immediate Enlightenment Sample Booklet*, or download or
subscribe to *The Supreme Master Ching Hai News* available in eBook or printable format, or simply
browse the sites' contents online.

Supreme Master Television

Info@SupremeMasterTV.com

Tel: 1-626-444-4385

Fax: 1-626-444-4386

http://www.suprememastertv.com/

Supreme Master Television goes GLOBAL on NOV. 16, 2007
Launching on 10 NEW Satellite Platforms!
Enjoy positive, inspirational and entertaining programs
With over 30 languages and subtitles!
Free-to-Air Satellite TV channel
Also LIVE online www.SupremeMasterTV.com

Inspired by the dogs
Compiled by:
The Supreme Master Ching Hai

Cameramen:
Supreme Master Ching Hai, Crystal Vo, Victor Ngo, T. June, Thomas Lux, Steven André, Danny Vu

Design and Layout:
Annie Yu, Nadir Yen, Chien Wei Ba-Li, Kim (Formosa); Jackie (Hsihu)

Graphic Design:
Gary Lai, Nadir Yen, Yu Hui-Chun, Wang Bor Tang (Formosa); Sofia, Jackie (Hsihu)

Copy Proofreading:
Lynn McGee, Jane Chu, Wenqing Li (USA); Becky Chen, Sun Wang, (Formosa);
Clair, Moon (Hsihu)

Publisher
The Supreme Master Ching Hai International Association Publishing Co., Ltd.
No 236 Soungshan Road, Taipei, Formosa, R. O. C.
Tel: 886-2-87873935
Fax: 886-2-87870873
www.smchbooks.com

The Supreme Master Ching Hai©2007
First Edition First Print: February 2007
First Edition Second Print: July 2007
First Edition Thrid Print: November 2007
Printed in Formosa
ISBN: 978-986-6895-08-1

Alternative Living

We Pray for You

Change Your Life
Change Your Heart
Change Your Diet

♥⸺♥

No more killing
Be healthy and loving

Save our Lives! We Love You

Examples of nutritious, life saving food:

Foods	Protein Concentration (Percentage by Weight)
Tofu (from soya)	16 %
Gluten (from flour)	70 %
Corn	13 %
Rice	8.6 %
Soy beans, kidney beans, chick peas, lentils, etc.	10 - 35 %
Almonds, walnuts, cashews, hazel nuts, pine nuts, etc.	14 - 30 %
Pumpkin seeds, sesame seeds, sunflower seeds, etc.	18 - 24 %

- Concentrated multi-vitamin tablets/capsules are also a good source of vitamins, minerals and anti-oxidants.
- Fruits and vegetables are full of vitamins, minerals and anti-oxidants and contain high-quality fiber for maintaining good health and a long life.
- The recommended daily allowance: 50 grams of protein (Average adult).
- Calcium from vegetables is more absorbable than from cow's milk.

• To diminish the real threat of a worldwide pandemic from bird flu,
• To avoid the danger of mad cow disease (BSE) and pig disease (PMWS), etc.
• To stop the continuing gruesome sacrifice of billions of our sweet domestic animals, marine life and feathered friends daily,

It's wise to change to a vegetarian diet for good.

It's Health
It's Economy
It's Ecology
It's Compassion
It's Peace
It's Noble

Long Life to You!

Thank You for Your Compassion

For more information, please refer to the websites listed below:
http://AL.Godsdirectcontact.org.tw/ or e-mail to AL@Godsdirectcontact.org
http://www.vegsoc.org/ http://www.vrg.org/ http://www.vegsource.com/
Supreme Master Television, airing only positive programming,
will bring a new dimension into your life.
Available worldwide as 24-hour live Internet TV at:
http://suprememastertv.com/webtv/